Contents

What are ramps and wedges?

A ramp is a slope for moving heavy things up and down. It is much easier to push something up a gentle ramp than up a steep one.

What Do
RAMPS AND WEDGES
Do?

Heinemann
LIBRARY

David Glover

www.heinemann.co.uk/library
Visit our website to find out more information about Heinemann Library books.

To order:
 Phone 44 (0) 1865 888066
Send a fax to 44 (0) 1865 314091
 Visit the Heinemann Bookshop at www.heinemann.co.uk/library to browse our
catalogue and order online.

First published in Great Britain by Heinemann Library,
Halley Court, Jordan Hill, Oxford OX2 8EJ, part
of Harcourt Education. Heinemann is a registered
trademark of Harcourt Education Ltd.

Editorial: Clare Lewis and Katie Shepherd
Design: Victoria Bevan and Q2A Creative
Illustrations: Barry Atkinson (pp11, 12, 19) and Tony
Kenyon (pp5, 9)
Picture Research: Mica Brancic
Production: Helen McCreath
Printed and bound in China by WKT Company
Limited

10 digit ISBN 0 431 06405 9
13 digit ISBN 978 0 431 06405 5
10 09 08 07 06
10 9 8 7 6 5 4 3 2 1

British Library Cataloguing in Publication Data
Glover, David
What do ramps and wedges do? - 2nd Edition
621.8
A full catalogue record for this book is available from
the British Library.

Acknowledgements
The publishers would like to thank the following for
permission to reproduce photographs: Trevor Clifford
pp1, 4, 5, 12, 13, 14, 18; Zefa pp6, 10; Jess Stock/
TSW p7; Sue Cunningham p9; J Ringland/TRIP
p11; Leonard Lee Rue/Bruce Coleman Ltd p15;
Colorsport pp8, 16, 17; Mary Evans Picture Library
p20; Robin Smith/TSW p21.

Cover photograph reproduced with permission of
Alamy.

The publishers would like to thank Angela Royston for
her assistance in the preparation of this book.

Every effort has been made to contact copyright
holders of any material reproduced in this book. Any
omissions will be rectified in subsequent printings if
notice is given to the publishers.

The paper used to print this book comes from
sustainable resources.

Any words appearing in the text in bold, **like this**, are
explained in the Glossary

FACT FILE Less effort

When you push something along a ramp it goes up gradually. You use less effort than when you lift the load straight up into the air.

A wedge is a small ramp that you can move. It is easy to slide a wedge under a door. The wedge **jams** the door open with a large force.

Zig-zags

It is hard work to climb a steep hill. You have to lift your body a long way with each step. A **zig-zag** path up a hillside takes you steadily to the top. You have to walk further than if you go straight up, but each step is easier.

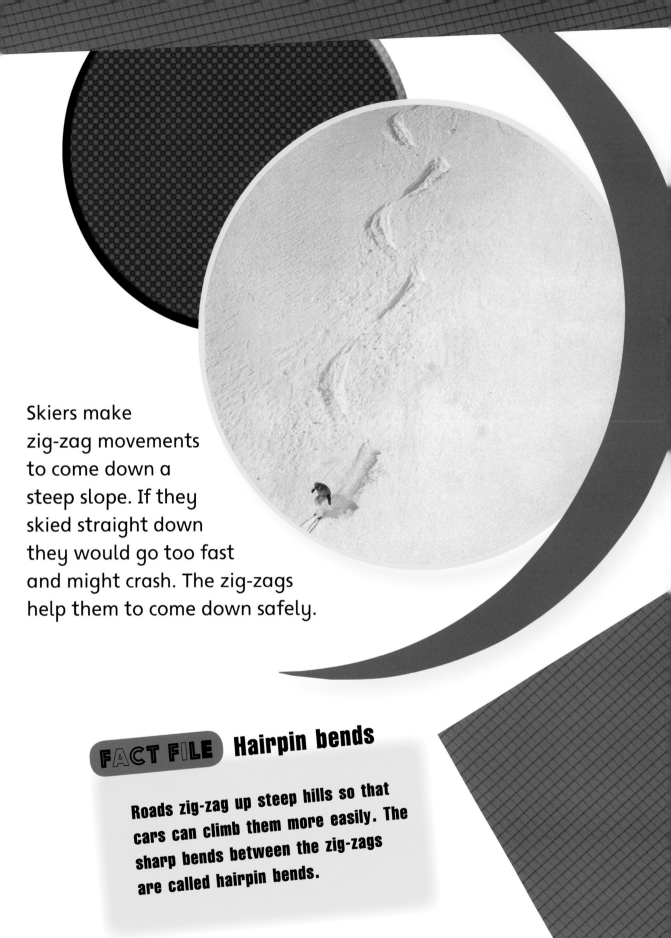

Skiers make zig-zag movements to come down a steep slope. If they skied straight down they would go too fast and might crash. The zig-zags help them to come down safely.

Blocks and chocks

Athletes use wedge-shaped blocks at the start of a race. They are called starting blocks, and they help the runners to push themselves off to a quick start.

This man is using metal wedges to split a block of stone. When he hammers the wedges into the stone, the wedge shape makes the stone split.

Chocks away!

Chocks were placed under the wheels of aeroplanes. They are wedges which stopped the plane from moving until the pilot was ready. When he wanted to take off, he shouted "Chocks away!"

Chocks away !

Axes and ploughs

An axe is a sharp metal wedge that is fixed to a handle. The handle lets you swing the axe head to hit a log with great force. The sharp wedge shape of the axe cuts into the wood and splits it apart.

Farmers use **ploughs** to turn the soil. A plough has blades that cut into the soil. These blades are metal wedges. They make lines called **furrows**. This tractor is pulling a plough with several blades.

Knives and scissors

When you cut a carrot with a knife, the blade works as a wedge. The sharp edge of the blade is very thin. It cuts easily into the carrot. The knife blade gets thicker away from the sharp edge. It forces the carrot apart.

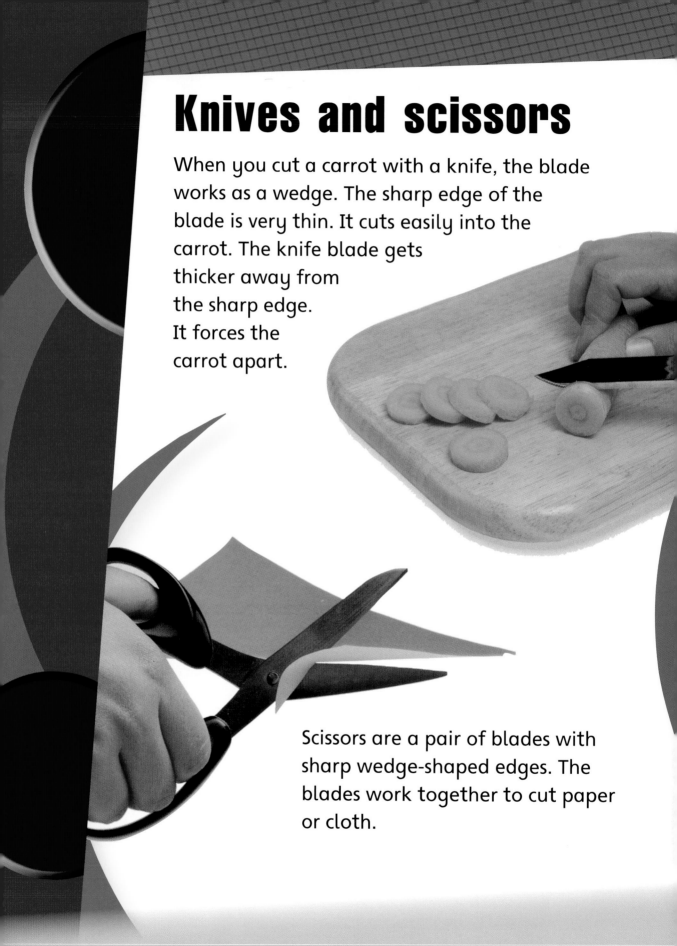

Scissors are a pair of blades with sharp wedge-shaped edges. The blades work together to cut paper or cloth.

FACT FILE Hedge trimmers

A hedge trimmer has lots of wedge-shaped blades. A motor moves the blades backwards and forwards at high speeds.

Secateurs are powerful scissors with a curved blade. They are used to cut twigs and branches.

Teeth

Feel the shape of your front teeth. They are wedges with sharp edges. You use these teeth to cut and bite your food. You can feel how they work when you take a bite from an apple.

Rats and mice have sharp incisor teeth for nibbling and gnawing their food. The beavers that live in North America can cut through tree trunks with their powerful wedge-shaped teeth. Beavers use the wood they cut to build their river homes.

FACT FILE Cutting teeth

The eight teeth at the front of your mouth are called incisors. The word "incisor" means cutter.

Giant jumps

This water skier is jumping off a ramp. The skier comes up to the ramp at high speed. The slope of the ramp lifts her into the air.

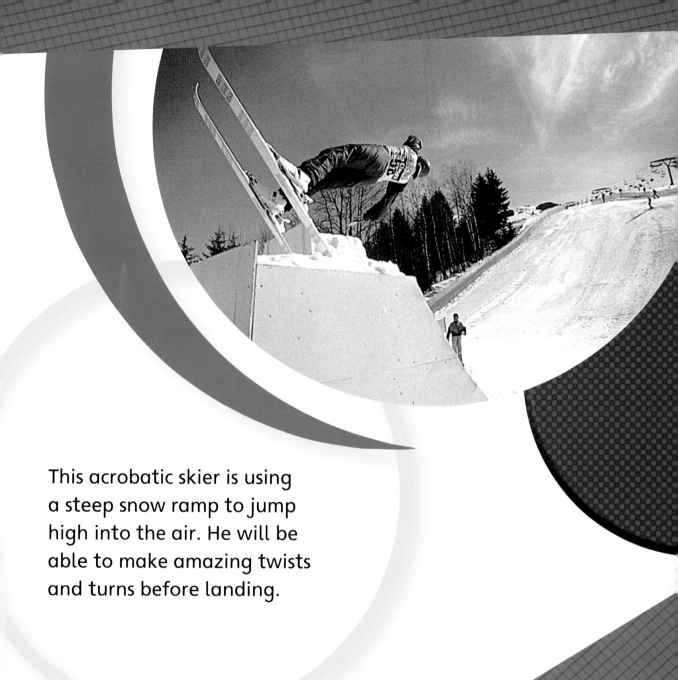

This acrobatic skier is using a steep snow ramp to jump high into the air. He will be able to make amazing twists and turns before landing.

FACT FILE Ski jumps

An expert water skier can jump half the length of a football pitch.

Zip it up!

It is almost impossible to close a zip without the **slider**. Two wedges inside the slider press the teeth together when you zip it up. A third wedge pushes the teeth apart when you pull the slider down.

The teeth on a zip are shaped so that they fit together, one after the other. A bump on one tooth fits into a dent on the next tooth.

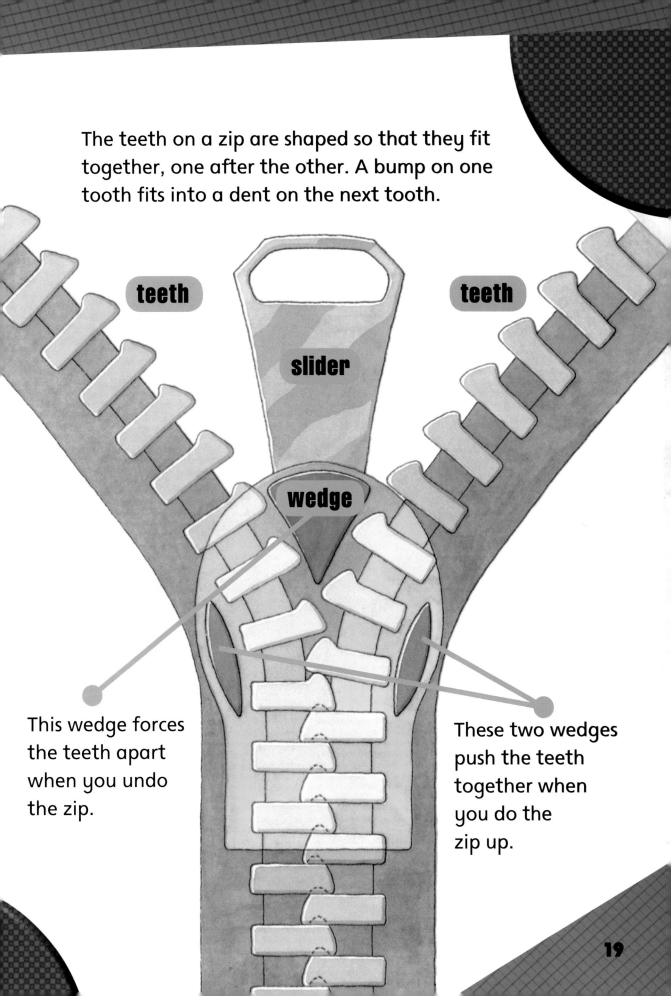

teeth

teeth

slider

wedge

This wedge forces the teeth apart when you undo the zip.

These two wedges push the teeth together when you do the zip up.

Slides and rides

Some of the most exciting fairground rides are slopes that you slide down at great speed.

Water splashes like this were popular 100 years ago. They are still great fun today. A rope pulls the car to the top of the slope and then lets the car go.

On a roller coaster your car is pulled to the top of a steep slope by a powerful engine. Then you rush down the slope on the other side. It is both frightening and exciting at the same time!

Activities

Testing a ramp

1. Make a ramp by balancing one end of a board on some books.
2. Tie a thread or string around a thick book.

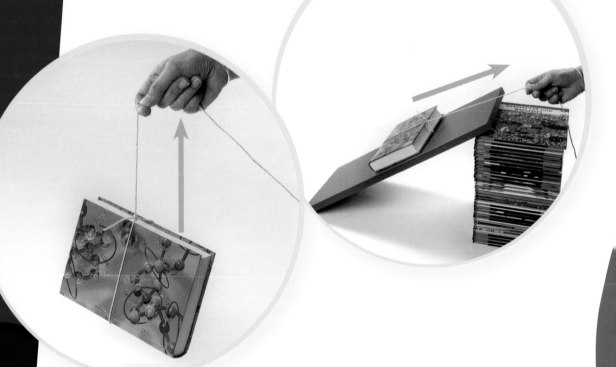

3. Pull the book up the ramp.
4. Now lift the book up in the air using the string. Which is easier – lifting the book or using the ramp?

See page 5 to find out why.

What makes the best door-stop?

1. Open a door. Put a heavy book against the bottom of the door.
2. Can you shut the door?

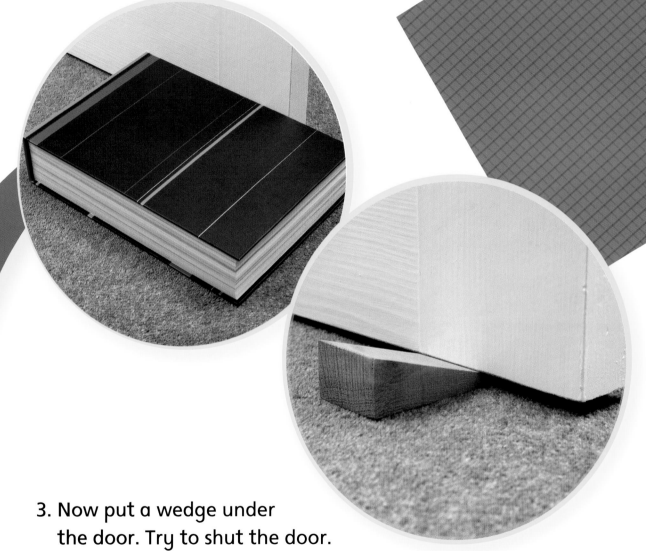

3. Now put a wedge under the door. Try to shut the door.
4. Which door-stop works best?

See page 5 for an explanation.

Glossary

chocks   wedge-shaped blocks for putting under wheels to stop them turning

effort   the pushing, pulling or turning force you must make to move something

furrows   the straight cuts or grooves in the ground that ploughs make as they turn the soil

jam   to block or wedge in one place

motor   the part of a machine that makes it go. Some motors are powered by electricity, others by petrol.

plough   machine with large blades pulled by a horse or a tractor. A farmer uses a plough to turn the soil in the fields.

secateurs   cutters that gardeners use to trim bushes and trees

slider   the part you move up and down to open and close a zip

zig-zag   line that turns to and fro

Index